Momentum

Also by Scott Thurston

Poems Nov 89 – Jun 91 (Writers Forum, London, 1991)
State(s) walk(s) (Writers Forum, London, 1994)
Fragments (The Lilliput Press, Norwich, 1994)
Sleight of Foot (with Miles Champion, Helen Kidd and Harriet Tarlo)
                (Reality Street Editions, London, 1996)
Two Sequences (RWC, Sutton, 1998)
Turns (with Robert Sheppard)
                (Ship of Fools/Radiator, Liverpool, 2003)
Of Utility (Spanner, Hereford, 2005)
Hold (Shearsman Books, Exeter, 2006)

Scott Thurston

Momentum

Shearsman Books
Exeter

Published in the United Kingdom in 2008 by
Shearsman Books Ltd
58 Velwell Road
Exeter EX4 4LD

ISBN 978-1-905700-32-5

Copyright © Scott Thurston, 2008.

The right of Scott Thurston to be identified as the author of this work has been asserted by him in accordance with the Copyrights, Designs and Patents Act of 1988. All rights reserved. No part of this publication may be reproduced, stored in a retrieval system, transmitted in any form or by any means, electronic, mechanical, photocopying, recording or otherwise, without the prior permission of the publisher.

Acknowledgements
Some of these poems have previously appeared in the following magazines: *Dusie, Erbacce, Fragmente, Great Works, Intercapillary Space, Lamport Court, Shadow Train, Shearsman, Skald, The Argotist Online, The Gig*. Many thanks to the editors.

Nine poems appeared in the Broken Compass Press Anthologies (0.1) and (0.2) in 2006. Thanks to Chris Brownsword.

Five poems appeared in *Slova Bez Hranic*, the anthology of the 2007 Words Without Borders festival in Olomouc, Czech Republic, in parallel with Czech translations. Thanks to Bob Hysek.

Contents

Singing Sensation   7

Separate Voices   41

Momentum   73

Singing Sensation

to Adrian Clarke

dashed singing sensation
      dares to incorporate a
robbery as if monotony
     an unfolded collar
of chambers beaten
     out on an anvil who
shouldered the wrong
      burden wants redressing
as a split bung type
     to the paradise of
another open matter
     offer pattern
regressing

yes it's chopped off
                      out of the ether
an oblong slide
                      into shaded polygon
a thick block
                      wedged into position
shifted over
                      determined minutiae
what magnifies
                      this ecstatic identification
as if a stone
                      hands over turns and
leaves

    cows and horses
               placed here equally
  asunder a redounded
                   sense of the outmoded
  categories the licenses
                     to print castellate
  the chimneys on the
                     horizon the simple point
  spits a loop of
             charcoal settling neatly
  the chance
               attendant on thought again

something happened
                        that tall day a
coach approaches out
                        of wistfulness
super sullen subtle
                        you might be on
a hiding to nothing
                        for tense means
an ingenuity that never
                        fails the fully
aligned arrangements
                        of emotion

the angle steeps
    up a rostrum
into a tense torso
    of reflections
a bum deal to
    recondite despite
the spilled guts
    of a singed contract
the seeming hopeless
    dumps into a skillet
marmoreal, funereal

wind proposes leaves
                       a tractable baffle a
front mazey with
                   starry points releases
you to what
              alternative two opposite
hoppers bottom
                  out a tactical battle
raising the meat
               gate

> what is it that it
> > answers to in me
> airline seating lines
> > paper through attention's
> thin folds hi-hat
> > sound hooks a hot spot
> to a point winking
> > at the brim of articulation
> how does it break
> > response into two
> does it start with
> > me or you?

the second before
     this leaving creature
sporting itself in
    joy now heads to
a passage of self
     destruction in an
instant all sport is
     ended the shocking
banality of its
   swiftness all too
unremittingly
   familiar

```
how to hang a
            split to pit that
wretched bulb
            bulging in one's eye
line head height
            bespoke addictions a simple worm
in the architecture
            love me love my hate dog
a sullen sip of
            disciplined testing
of a vintage
            vintage better bettered only the next
time around
```

toughen things
            into their special
apportioned proportion
                    a speck of timeless
dated innocent angst
                guides in dissolves to
a hair in the gate
                what are your bounds
your grounds so solid
                    to run your duty on
batch it hawk it
            quick
over the border

your hair
    as a blunt napkin
sawn in two
     to promote multiple rites
atop a carnage
     left a lot of wishful
thinking to be
     done a part to catch
lots of sensation
      duck ducts of consolatory
revelation

in the cramped
            geometric corridor your
space is uneased
            for a batted window sleep
slide off an incline
            in the glass house where
an alarm winking
            in the ground provokes a
depth your eased
            figure skated to a petrol
can that props
            the door in secure
lighting

no if what you
              think no if what
you if what you
              no feel in your
moving centre
              if you get grounded
nailed upon two
              pins for support
it don't knock you
              move you in your
centre moved
              and moving still

    her sparkling empathy
                          as we study bacon
a study of a dog
               where is he at
the beach he can
                  smell ice cream
everyone is ignoring
                     me trapped in a frame
like a basketball court
                 what have we bound
out of you two
             we and I in starry
perfection?

retune into
> tomorrow's morose remorse

I can feel it
> here taut in my moving

centre it
> snakes my wrist across my brow

tho' there is
> no need of external description

book it slap
> on a slab that fat

insensate chances
> > bore away

yesterday

place the head against
                        the graph and something else
begins to show up
                    the cap had to be shown
before it was
                removed aiming at the space
behind the head
                  holding still the texture
shows up the anti
                    glare coating on the spectacle
but speculates on
                a long process of recovery

take cover from
    my artificial intelligence
draw fire from
    a host of coasted gestures
sprung back to
    reveal a shipped resource
rapt in
   corrugated cargo hold flexible
storage inverts
    a new space outwards in
vents an attempted
    scan of the justified desserts
quality seconds

shapeless nothing
                    light flash off the top
of a brick wall
                recalls a walk where
time stood still
                a static atmosphere where
one's boundaries
                    start to expand, cause an
intrograde shifting
                      a current presence of past
life on a disused
                  railway track on a winter's
afternoon

    plea for realism that
                      all the values reflect
    only a part of
                the larger world we
    live in check
                the upbeat matrix where
    no human assessors
                      are necessary for a sudden
    shudder breaks a
                bespoke statement we know
    where this is coming
                    from but how do we know
    when we are doing well?

    that cool garden
               becomes an arena
of force for warring
                    clans amongst nature between
city streets now no
                  more nor less horrific than
the transmissions
                what is permanently temporary
is the smell
         the way it wraps its map
way back
            in the ancient fledgling mind
no better
        no worse

    he is gone
             at the exact moment
    that we
          recognised him his sacrifice
    making him
            something more than he
    had been for
            us when he sat straightforwardly
    daily on the
            dresser his uniqueness
    is also ours
            tho' it may take us
    all our time
            to find it

that wasn't me
               in this perturbable schedule
a host of glowing
                 lights dispersed through a
body taints the
                 overactive gland with a sharp
stain of movement
                 in here I've forgotten myself
already bound
                 to a hesitant world fallen
in with fortune's
                 partner to begin to admit
in fact that
                 it was me

red pen on
           red paper your hand
extends into
           a rock more contrast
is required
           when the invitation came
when least
           expected shine on the
crystalline
           line of interhuman form
you wish
           for what you get

```
impression in the mirror –
                    a cast of lines converges
on a shattered visage
                    makes marks in a moving
time of reflection
                    cannot be caught exactly
knot in time
              to preserve in us a fulsome
following taint
                 of the lone, level absolute
stretch for a
              way get clean away
today
```

eclipse infinity
     it is not you who are
not equal to it
     but it stands close to
a wall of sand
     light makes it through
water also into
     a tense still sound
welling could start
     from here reach the
perimeter view a
     new moral horizon

the earth still
                doesn't know how old
it is yet it
                ages terribly – that plaintive
night cry
                above what has remained
a coast
                for a while at least knows
as much
                and as little as we settle
in a field
                of moving silence

what you can be
             is not philosophy
what you can't
             change entreats itself
to hold eye contact
                    stand its ground
and move with you
                  it is not that
simple but leaves
                 an open pressure
makes monumental
                    a tiny human
gesture

in different will
                    to noise responsibility
again provokes
                    in the enclosed space
who dares to
                    step outside their bounds
to collapse into
                    the screened environment
swallow it like
                    grit to a defensive pill
bitter to know
                    this is the distracted
numbness you
                    prefer

what is it that it
             fires up in me
in this difficult
             passage or not a passage
but a stable
             set of distinguishable
circumstances
             acting on which a twist
provokes another
             dimensional view
the split hair
             a reed quivering between
reality and
             imagination

into my shattered
                   song bring down a
shaft of crimson
                   light to break weight
of this solemn
                   compact against my heir's
self-breath
                   worm-suns benighted catch
back a staunch
                   breath redoubled effort
breaks into song
                   all over again for the
now and then

Separate Voices

    the small
              support the large in a
    forest where
              another law is apparent
    when I stop
              here I literally get off
    become object
              of another world's subjects
    the bleached
              logs spin wink out
    of sun's spot
              a sudden immersion
    bordering on
              disappearance

the totally uncompromising
                    stance comprises a promise
to a tone
            spread out in subtle rings
of selfishness
                it bangs a head broad open
cuts against
                a star board right for
bloody
            intricacies simple sudden a
shower
            caught you again for your
deep deliberate
                    colours tacked to a mast

I adore you
            so much that I completely
forgot about
            you lying there between
the sheets
            a resurgence of a split
glyph turned
            out of sidings anonymous
in a place
            where grit in one's eye
turns to jewelled
                    beauty a fractured tenderness
a blackbird
            singing

being beguiled
    by the surface of perfection
belies a deep
    dissatisfaction that one gives
you your easy
    surface easily and yet
this one you
    find intolerable because it
reminds you
    of the depth you crave
your need
    without being trapped by
it to disperse
    those lines a little wider
till it hears
    you

what are the
            edges so tied up tight in
me that when
            I turn the page turn over
in bed I arrive
            on another plane of
consciousness
            and it breaks to suggest out
of a patterned
            barricade those gleaming surfaces
is it living well
            to shine so bright or is a hoax
concealed is the
            work boiled down to its essentials
or is it the last
            cracked remaining residue
of thought?

make a drive hole
                         down into history as age's
becoming breaks
                         the ties between the root
and the head of the
                         crop the paradoxical gap
is an opening out
                         where the dream turns from
the surface back
                         into a future narrative a
wager for knowing
                         or a relationship to knowing
a sudden beguiling
                         harmony between the train
on the track
              the truck
on the bridge

```
are they all
            prisoners in the medium
in which they
            live whether it be the
fabric of labour
            or simply light sucking
air a dazzling
            baffle of wings addresses
the gradient
            gradual reminiscences coalesce
about a refuge
            on a cliff solid markings
of gendered
            territory only out of
kilter with the
            odd sharp jabs and tussles
as the air
            ruffles the surface again
```

idę za głosem
           przez dom – nie jest cicho
czerwony
        na ścianie, serce jest na
dywanie
        a skrzydła na krześle. Gramy
tu przez
        całą noc nic nie mówimy nie
jest cicho
        cały świat jest blisko nie
słyszy o czym
        mówimy

I follow the voice through the whole house – it is not quiet. There is red on the wall, a heart on the carpet and some wings on a chair. We play here through the whole night. We don't say anything, it is not quiet. The whole world is close but it can't hear what we are saying.

no put an end
              to it this cheap lottery
of accidents turning
                  the year back on itself
to compare how
                many bought it on this
day back then
              to minimize hope
a lesser death
              count makes us safer
but never questioning
                    the square root of what
is wrong why
            we get in the car blameless
emerge nameless

                your pure joy
                                in being shines through
                in the old
                                photos – you knew how to look
                or not to look
                                at the camera but whatever
                pose there is
                                I can sense luminous moments:
                the sun on snow
                                as you feed your dog.
                A piece
                        of wall looks suddenly real as if
                it hasn't changed
                                and exposes how you stay
                in and of history
                                except your eyes blazing with
                utter presence
                                in 1934, in Poland

    in another country
                    regaining control of one's
    body is what
           regaining knowledge of the
    language is what
                regaining control of one's
    language is what
                language am I hurt in
    what new rhythm
                  enters here obliterates habit
    which then slowly
                  tragically re-establishes itself
    relishes itself
               what regains control requires
    control
         in another language

is there a coin
>>that spun once to fall
on the side of
>>hard lineaments expressed
as a set of
>>benches ranged around a
tough centre?
>>there are gestures which
break out
>>across this space with
terrifying compass
>>the dance of a red flag
suspended from
>>the ceiling completes the
violent beauty

    your congress
                dispatches me once again
    to a daydream
               that reveals a dispute gone
    bitterly destructive
                was simply long held
    anger needing
                to be listened to: Lovelace's
    offer of service
               in return for trust long gone
    I dream again
               of when the congress of the
    cow becomes
               the congress of the crow

'characterising your location
                on an implementation staircase'
the changing room
                changes you feeds back to
your personal
                furniture your whole inclusion
depends upon
                a body gesture in time
a turn towards
                or away, a pause to wait
for you or
                to leave how lightly to go
to stay to
                lodge in time and space
how easy is
                it to go far away today
another day

that I don't really
           have a sense of my will
as if the things
           which happen, which I do
were offerings
           which I accepted rather than
objects I sought
           like being on a track
laid out long
           before you but is this a
great groove
           in the sky which draws
all into it or
           the rough historical contingencies
of chance
           and habit?

an addiction
                returns full force after a respite
I get turned into
                a side line a slide show projecting
what has been
                neglected or even entirely
forgotten what
                defences or what improvements
but that can't
                help but form a feint to the more
powerful pose
                that dictates virtue needs its
shadows awful
                ruse that runs me back to dip
again

indentity is
            my impression backing
into sleep
            to meet a sharp scarp of
absorbing
            resistance brings my you
back to your
            my troubled over determined
patterns of
            rest abounding in repose
to determine
            us is to rerun us
determinedly
            out of town out of night

when you have
                nowhere to write you don't
write you breathe
                in a manner of instilled
instincts of installed
                accents troubled at every
turn of the knife
                edge of judgement heretofore
one neither
         gives up nor gains anything
noticing
        the length of the inhale
the length
      of the exhale

I've inoculated it
            I've made it safe with
a dose of its own
            toxic medicine – practice
and discipline bind
            to the receptor heads
and it's a dead
            duck. Over-confident perhaps
overwhelmed to
            start so suddenly so brashly
against the ranked
            opposition bristling with
deadly spikes ranged
            along an eerie sub-sonic
sub-atomic shore

back slap to break
              back an attack a return
to the break beat
              echoes through yesterday's
kitchen a dull foam
              starts to adhere clouds
over a film but
              another layer accrues where
the note is
              interrupted by a view through
the chink
              it is both and not where I
started from
              forgetting recollection merely
evokes it here
              right before my eyes

    the astonishing pleasure
                      of another cup of cappuccino
    following on from the
                      first – the object restored
    to itself renewed
                      recovered in joy and yet
    already the foam
                      contracts the bubbles winking
    at the brim start
                      to go out pocking craters
    in the chocolate
                      crusting once again restoring
    the solid ghost
                      of endlessly lost potential
    hopelessly regained
                      in a gulf of sorrow

telling the time
             by till receipts traced across
a city orients
             my purchasing power – little
disasters bob up
             everywhere: nature scoffs at
the landing stage
             wrecked, sunken in the estuary.
That pontoon
             floated with hope in an earlier
poem unlike
             this one which has already
forgotten its
             ending: not on my abandoned
watch

    clutched in the human
                    forest the fronds of pikes
  held aloft become
               like the sweetest blossom –
  thank humanity
               for holding me in enchanted
  boundaries an open
               forest moving as a heart
  beat wept to
            spit on a open wound – yes
  the turn to
             violence again – a punctured
  dreamspace
             only elevates the next version
  ever nobler
             ever more coming back

a knife amnesty
                of double edged words
who would hold
                it up to glance off
and back hand
                your friends in safe
in the knowledge
                striking out always looks
back into your
                own flesh til nothing
beside remains
                only the blade tall and
shining burning
                over the desert

          that something has
                              a form and is a form
          beckons me one
                         over a bell tolling in
          the distance
                       gives form to air to time
          reassuring that
                         my trials are really nothing
          substantial nor
                          serious not even missiles
          shot over
                    borders can change that
          really
                can they?

the form
            I make in a tight spot
impresses
            a dent in the cosmos
which in
            turn becomes a constraint
a mould
            a straitjacket til I move
again and
            in moving alter the mould
break its
            prison til I coalesce
back into
            the captured angle keep it
moving
            still stop start moving
again

```
that ostensive
                that designates a boundary
    that you fall
                foul of quickly to dream
    of a burnt
                setting a suddenly won
    over know
                ledge of coruscating
    cruelty of
                unlimited intelligence spin
    it call it
                require it brought to book
    to control
                its uneven presence
```

the science
            of literature cannot be
constrained
            from the technologies that
counter it
            to cast a descriptive system
to reliably
            predict predicates to set in
open war
            an opposing proposal to support
troubled
            response ability becomes a right
to aim at
            repeatedly

    take a cross
               section through a wall
    provoke a human
                    figure to be enabled there
    moving parallel
               to banisters on a staircase
    landing what
                this exercise proposes is a scheme
    of a trap
             a sketch of a structure
    for escape
              that neither invites nor
    deters
            perpetually

capture your
                hand on a handsfree
mobile post
            it on the net what has
changed in
              the transmission: digital
corruption
              splits porn from graphic
you have
           turned your hand from
worse before
            but still feel as if
you have
             given a self away
again

Momentum

How might we embody
an opposing hope
in a simple movement
phrase?

—Edwin Salter 'Working with Movement'

what does it belong
     to if it doesn't belong
to you
  momentum a wave through a
body
  makes some starting places dart
and smart
   a glistening ache immaterial
at last
  gasp a stage to mount a
hope that
   there is no remedy for all
that trust

this parallel
        dance in a tradition
cages in
        parodic circles your self
circumscribing
        encircles you encloses you
in a repetitive
        orbit a puncture wound
into which
        you ceaselessly pour
and recast
        your dark materials
in your own
        image

four people long
            dead in a ring around
me appear first
            in recognisable guises from
the old snap
            shots then transform into
something
            ideal without being abstract their
hands stretched
            out towards me the already
no more
            becomes the already there
in the dance

how to organise
    a body without organs
you use
  the energy you have already
moving
   so you don't have to start
from scratch
    every time expand out pick
up speed
   then slow it right back
down so
   it is internal feel movement
re-organising
    your body without organs
within organs
   without

can't you fake it
            showing up at the page
for a deep
            sexual core burning through you
the school
            of involuntary impressions becomes
a rebounding
            curse to split productivity from
authenticity
            when all that you want is
held in
        a bowl all ready to tilt
and spill
        its contents to find its
own level

the unwitting
            shadow is one that doesn't
dance but
            stiffens in a grip across belly
and throat
            and can barely shift weight
in a sway
            here at home we polarise
what otherwise
            disperses in the public fountain
it is another
            version of a practice parallel
like a moiré
            effect where objects change
into spiritual
            matter

dismantle the
            solemn inner book of unknown
assemblages
            of signs – can you think with
water?
        Finding a book in a dream
that you
        didn't write kinetically links
the unlinkable
            connects your feet to a
bayonet
        thrust through the throat that
you didn't
        make let alone talk about
ever again

a defensive jaw
    head held in position starts
to soften
   towards journey's end in me
a stitch of
    tension about this charge
and that one
     leaves me reeling: is it
really they
    who have changed so
suddenly
   or is it me now more open
in the thrall
    of momentum?

if a brick
    hits the window behind
my head
    where am I? All a flow
til a sudden
    sharp staccato shot catches
a tension.
    If an eight year old
threw it
    through my head where
would I
    be: in this chaos
what can
    I not see?

how to take
	responsibility where is the
root the entry
	point there isn't one
it's ground
	less but not unforgivable
that a bus
	becomes a stand-in for the
social wall
	as it knelt vulnerably
at a stop:
	how to interpret this most
sincere
	and sinister of messages
how to act

when my paralysis
    is so evident – a dropped
ticket yesterday
    and a broken picture frame in a
bag on the
    same patch of stairs today what
symbols
    am I ignoring at my own risk
what ignores
    me as it prepares to float
carry
  engulf me in itself which is
my own
    my only flood the turn
of the wave

after
       the dance in the middle
of the night
              I feel a hollow along
the length
           of my spine as if the bed
has rolled
           into a tube beneath me
lifting me
           up my face feels stretched
as if by
        gravity the sounds of birds
outside
        curiously amplified then I
fall
    back down

Experiments conducted with glass and perspex were unsuccessful. Finally, a purposebuilt 'collar' that sits around the text of the open book has served to alleviate a number of problems, not least that of the fingers encroaching upon the image. The collar serves as an extension to the hands, undetected by the scanner's software. Even pressure can now be applied to the book, preventing indentations that would previously be detected on the final image. The collar also reduces the risk of damage to delicate volumes and secures pages that would normally move without the use of the hands. In terms of aesthetics the collar has also improved the appearance of the image by masking unsightly blotches caused by extensive foxing or stains caused by careless readers. The resulting image is framed by a white border hiding the sides and edges of the book.

If you search for
something good for you
to be tilled,
get nailed.

She was close
to Bisesa. She
could not challenge,
you must call on
being honed over

generations

Experiments conducted with glass and perspex were unsuccessful. Finally, a purposebuilt 'collar' that sits around the text of the open book has served to alleviate a number of problems, not least that of the fingers encroaching upon the image. The collar serves as an extension to the hands, undetected by the scanner's software. Even pressure can now be applied to the book, preventing indentations that would previously be detected on the final image. The collar also reduces the risk of damage to delicate volumes and secures pages that would normally move without the use of the hands. In terms of aesthetics the collar has also improved the appearance of the image by masking unsightly blotches caused by extensive foxing or stains caused by careless readers. The resulting image is framed by a white border hiding the sides and edges of the book.

If you search for
something good for you
to be tilled,
get nailed.

She was close
to Bisesa. She
could not challenge,
you must call on
being honed over

generations

where is it
		called longing I want to
hold on I
		can't bear to hold on
exchange
		a torpid density for a lost
release
		called to account for expensive
shame
		spirit matters in another's
waste
		where it is called belonging
I lie
	back use whomever is around
me to
		climb out of the pit

wind moves
    everything no longer
kept in thrall
    by projections of the ideal
know that
    pain and suffering are there
too across
    the margin of contingencies
so much
    is still here for a little bit
of time
    in its pure state leaves
moving
    light water falling metal
barricade
    collapses

your message
         to sort him out
to sort
     her out I reply no
they are
     not problems they are
humans
     you reply okay they are
humans
     but not sorry where
does it
     line up in the indeterminate
tone of
     mature immature intimacy
have I
     shouted out of you
echo of
     virtual self?

they have begun
           to dazzle speechlessly what
is being ex
           changed here where I change
places give
           up my seat to take one among you
finding a new
           kind of creativity what is it
I have made
           have I made this community
or has it
           just allowed me to exist in
richness
           perpetuity?

lost progress
            to the point where the
figure takes up
            residence – your story was
great in itself
            but not as you intended so
absorbed
            in your conception you had no
idea it
      could be read so differently
but then I
            also began to doubt whether
I'd grasped it
            well enough at all
to start with

lost perfection
                again haunts an admirer
on the sexual
                stage where my two new
companions
                shadow me gently bringing
out what
                as we triangulate our positions
to delve
                into what slant chance pours
on tour
                chasten us hasten us
begin again
                in the now and then
again

will I find
　　　　　　you in time what
　　　constitutes it
　　　　　　　what is it constituted by
　　　extreme
　　　　　　simplicity makes me a force
　　　field
　　　　　of energy nothing but a
　　　breeze
　　　　　　over stuff I'm changing my
　　　shape
　　　　　they keep the windows
　　　locked
　　　　　　and the doors shut

pour falls to
                flow into respect only
the next day
                following a room full
of bodies
                intense questioning difficult
answers
            you are bent into another
shape
        not by another's administering
touch
        in the field nor by your
own
     but by the blank screened
enormity
         of construction

art gives
        nothing shelter in this
moment
        of departure a bivouac in
the corner
        of the building site or
a tent
        by the railway barely transitive
presences
        not harmful but destroyed
with
        apparent impunity over again
the end
        of some utterly subjugated
zone zero
        tolerance

in winter in
          the body of a spring
something
          remembers something feeling
not fear
          in your solitude a body
passing
          unseen to an authentic
scene
          dancing alone in the upper
room
          the music barely audible
your
          chest thrust forward shapes
some
          thing shapes some thing
shapes
          something

before you
            sign you know your
signal
        taking your arms in hand
handing
            you a sign that doubles you
up you
            in turn reshape me suddenly
taking
            hold of shield and sword
releases
            a succession of stalking
instants
            brilliant you healed
in a word

to impress
           upon the seal of it then
your signet
           ring which I now wear
bent to
           your shape it slips round
my finger
           will I give it up for a
year to
           find out what it really is
so much
           for what is essential
so much
           for what is necessary

you behind
            glass on an island hold
a moving
            surface a surfeit of
supplication
            applied it takes the whole
person away
            to listen to the waves all
day for what
            comes to land or what unfolds
landing
        for you nothing announces
peace
      you who would not be forgiven
outside
          the institutions

I forget
        repeating myself what is it
that really
        separates us virtual wave
of emotion
        serial encounters figure against
ground
        ground back into ground the
specific
        despair of a poem recuperated
as the
        general joy of the sequence
the book
        is not essential it just
affords
        occasional glimpses of

this time
        the sign flies overhead
smashes
        in the road we turn stare
move on
        tell the police the message
interpreted
            cycles anger cycles fear cycles
forgive
     the only way across as we
stand
   looking at one another on the
other
     side of the road

in the heat
        of the heart's art
what it
        can be trusted when it
is over
        it is never over broken
voices
        breaking me into construction
rest
    your weary heart wszystko
możliwe
        nothing forces us to think
signs
    in relief at an ending

Notes

p. 52   i.m. Róża Skopek (1913-2001)

p. 102 for St. Dwynwen, Ynys Llanddywn, Ynys Môn

p. 105 wszystko możliwe: everything possible